colour CALLIGRAPHY

by Barbara Bundy

ISBN 1 871517 05 2

Osmiroid Creative Leisure Series

About the Author

Barbara Bundy is a freelance calligrapher and heraldic artist. Although initially self-taught, she has since furthered her calligraphic training with Gaynor Goffe, Sam Somerville and Thomas Ingmire.

She is a member of the Society of Scribes and Illuminators (SSI) and the Heraldry Society. Her professional work involves occasional civic and ecclesiastical commissions but mainly experimental projects requiring interpretive designs.

She enjoys teaching all aspects of calligraphy and heraldic art and is an SSI approved tutor. Her courses for students of all abilities are based in and around Winchester, Hampshire, where she lives with her husband and two daughters.

She is also the author of "The Art of Illuminated Lettering and Heraldry", the successful companion to this book, published by Berol Ltd.

Calligraphic designs for the cover and pages 30–59 are works by the author.

©**Berol Corporation, Berol Ltd., Oldmedow Road, Kings Lynn, Norfolk PE30 4JR. Tel: 0553 761221. 1989. Reprinted 1990/1**

CONTENTS

INTRODUCTION

We live in a world saturated with colour. Every day as we wake, light and colour flood our homes, exciting our eyes and uplifting our spirits. Who has not been elated by a spring morning and the prospect of warm sunlight, bright green grass, a tree heavy with pink blossom and white clouds scudding across a clear blue sky?

Colour has such significance in our lives. Have you noticed how young children love and respond to vivid colours? Offer toddlers bright paint and they will just as happily scoop it up to eat as daub it on paper with their fingers!

In our surroundings at home, in the clothes we wear and the cars we buy, the choice of colour reflects our personalities. We all respond to colours in different ways. Some prefer the safety of quiet colours, like greys and beige. Others delight in wearing outrageous colour schemes, sometimes to attract attention, sometimes as a means of self-expression.

Learning how to use colour is fun and there are so many opportunities for us to make colour decisions. New tiles for the bathroom, paint for the front door, a new shirt – these are examples when a little colour knowledge enables us to select colours with confidence.

We are all potential artists, whether we paint with pigments, wool, fabrics or words. I enjoy "painting with words" and I use colour to shape and emphasize my chosen texts. Every piece of work is rather like a voyage of discovery, experimenting with colour to create a pleasing and exciting design.

If you enjoy handwriting or have recently taken up calligraphy, then knowing something about colour will enable you to be more creative. I hope some of the ideas in this book will inspire you to experiment more freely and will encourage you to begin "looking" – really looking at the world of colour around you.

did the wond'rous
speech and sped
embracing magic
and to colou

COLOUR LANGUAGE

The Spectrum

We need light in order to see colour, and the brighter the light, the more vivid colour becomes. By contrast, at night or in a darkened room, we see little or no colour. The English physicist, Sir Isaac Newton, was the first person to explore the relationship between light and colour.

In 1676 he made the exciting discovery that a glass prism could disperse a beam of sunlight to create a series of different colours. He identified seven of them arranged in succession, just like those we see in a rainbow. He listed the colours as violet, indigo, blue, green, yellow, orange and red, and called this multicoloured band the *SPECTRUM.*

During the last century scientists were able to show that, of these colours, violet-blue, green and orange-red are the primary or basic spectrum colours. From these, secondary colours, cyan-blue, yellow and magenta-red can be created. These six colours are called the *BASIC CHROMATIC COLOURS.* Such pure colours are known as *HUES.*

This multi-coloured band of colour is called the Spectrum. The colours visible to the eye range from violet through blue and green to yellow and red.

The Primary and Secondary Colours

Now we are not all physicists like Sir Isaac Newton, but it is possible to match the spectrum colours with pigments in order to learn more about colour and how colours can be mixed. If you have a box of paints, you might like to paint your own colour wheel. Begin with just three colours– ideally, magenta-red, yellow and cyan-blue. Try mixing red with yellow to make orange, yellow and blue to make green and red and blue to make violet. We call magenta-red, yellow and cyan-blue the *PRIMARY COLOURS*.

By mixing these as described you will now see how to create the *SECONDARY COLOURS* – orange-red, green and violet-blue. Further mixing between primary and secondary colours creates *TERTIARY COLOURS*. The colour gradations are endless and you only need three colours to start. Coloured paper cut from magazines is another way of putting together a colour wheel.

By overlapping semi-circular filters – magenta, yellow and cyan blue, three new colours are created – orange-red, green and violet-blue.

Find the right colours to fit the spaces on the colour wheel.

Neutral Colours

The two other basic colours, which are crucial to us in creating a range of colour schemes, are the achromatic colours – *BLACK* and *WHITE*. These two colours belong to the group of *NEUTRAL* colours which include greys, beiges and creams. They have very little pure hue in them and make useful background colours for calligraphy. If you visit your local art shop and look at the range of papers, you will begin to appreciate the variety of neutral colours.

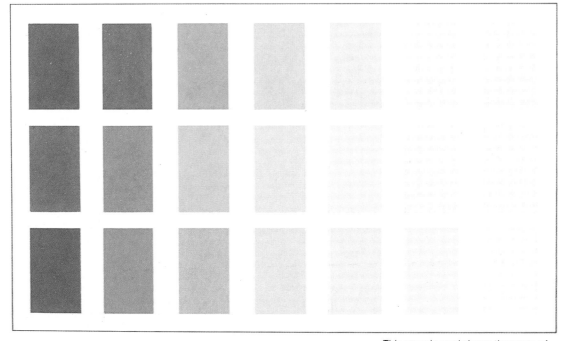

This sample card shows the range of tints which can be created from red.

Lemon, peach, pink, lime, lavender are all tints created by adding white to the basic colours.

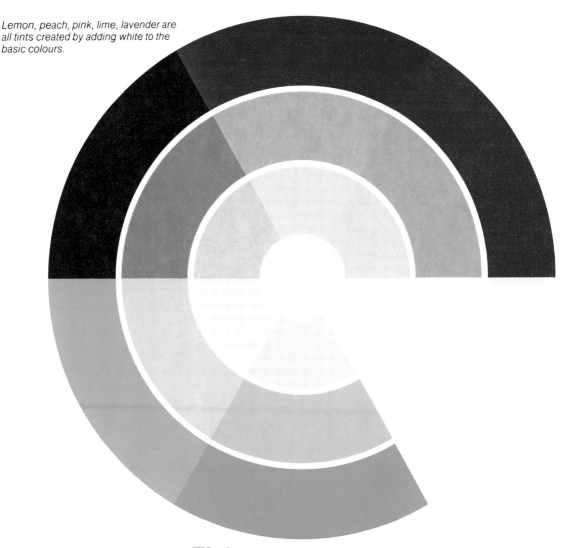

Tints

You may now be wondering how we arrive at the vast range of pastel colours. This is achieved by adding a small amount of white paint to each colour on the colour wheel. By increasing the amount of white paint, paler and paler colours will result. It is also possible with inks to add just water and make pale diluted colours. These pastel colours are called *TINTS*. By trying to mix pastel colours of your choice, you will become aware of all the subtleties available to you. Another idea you can try is overlapping tissue papers of varying colours. The semi-transparent effects give subtle combinations and help you make instant colour schemes.

Shades

Darker *SHADES* of the six basic colours can also be mixed simply by adding varying amounts of black. Too much black will very easily kill colours, and some artists prefer not to use black at all. If you try creating your own range of sombre colours, be careful to add only a tiny amount of black.

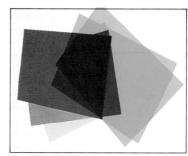

These overlapping acetate sheets create varying shades of brown at the centre.

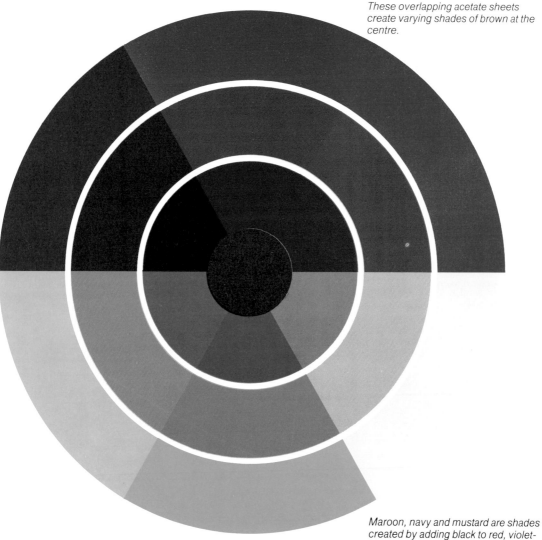

Maroon, navy and mustard are shades created by adding black to red, violet-blue and yellow respectively.

The Tone Scale – a useful exercise to try.

Tone

Shades of colours must not be muddled with colour *TONE*. This refers to the lightness or darkness of colours and can be best appreciated by looking at black and white photographs. A yellow dress for example will appear as pale grey, whilst violet curtains will look dark grey. By using black ink and diluting it gradually with water you can paint a *TONE SCALE*. This is a fairly demanding exercise but will greatly increase your knowledge of colour.

By comparing these two photographs, you will see how the colours appear either light, medium or dark in tone in the black and white photograph.

Harmony

We often look at room schemes, paintings or dress fabrics and admire the restrained use of colour, where a pleasing *HARMONY* is achieved. The colours have a subtle blending effect. Nothing is too obvious. We are just aware of gradual colour variations. If you select colours of similar tone or colours closely related on the colour wheel, you will also achieve this harmony. You can then adapt a similar scheme for your next piece of calligraphy.

Fabrics and papers collected from one section of the colour wheel create a harmonious scheme.

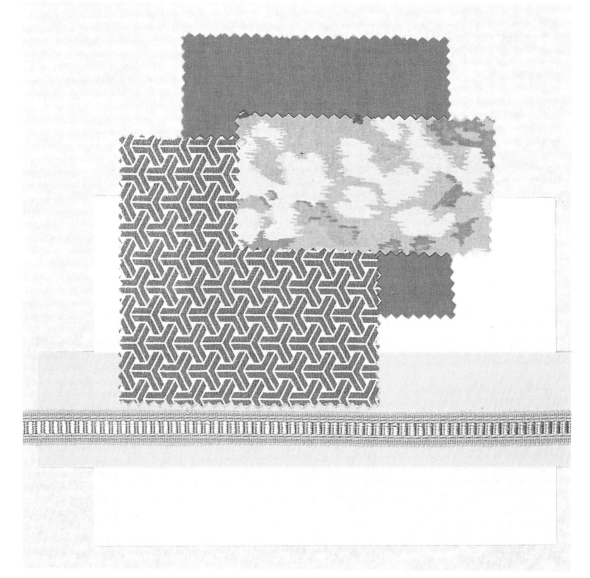

Contrasts

If you want to startle or make an impact with your designs you will need to use *CONTRASTS* of colour. Try using black on white or white on black for maximum tonal contrast, or choose colours found opposite each other on the colour wheel. These are called *COMPLEMENTARY* colours. Imagine a poster with a cyan-blue background. By choosing the complementary colour orange-red for your lettering you will create a very eye-catching design.

Warm and Cool Colours

As you become more colour-conscious, you will find certain colours seem ''warm'' while others appear ''cool''. Reds are warm, blues are cool. Yellow can be a warm golden colour if mixed with a little red or cool if a little blue is included, making it lime-coloured. Even shades of grey can be warm or cool, but you will need to be quite observant to distinguish these subtle variations.

Colour Symbolism

Finally, we all associate colour with emotions and events, sometimes without quite knowing why. As children we learn that black is worn for funerals and so we relate black to death. For many, red means danger or fire and white denotes cleanliness or purity. Attitudes to certain colours are often triggered by happy or disturbing events, and so turquoise might be a favourite colour for one person but upsetting for another. This use of *COLOUR SYMBOLISM* can play an interesting part in creating calligraphic designs. You may be able to think of other colour associations that could be useful.

TOOLS AND
TECHNIQUES

Once you have tried some of the colour exercises, you will be ready to use colour more effectively in your calligraphy designs. Initially, all you need to get started is a pen, ink and paper. Gradually you may want to buy additional items as your knowledge about calligraphy increases.

Pens

You will find the modern fountain pen a convenient writing tool for both handwriting and formal calligraphy. It provides a regular flow of ink and allows you to concentrate on letter shapes. The Osmiroid Calligraphy Pen is very suitable for beginners and it has the advantage of a wide range of interchangeable nibs, both for left and right-handers. Later on, as your expertise increases, you may want to try writing with dip pens, also produced by Osmiroid.

Eventually you may learn to cut and write with your own quill! These were in constant use throughout the Western world until Victorian times. All the early manuscripts were written with a variety of quills taken from swans, geese, turkeys, ducks and crows. Many professional calligraphers today prefer quills because of their unique, subtle qualities.

A selection of pens manufactured by Osmiroid, showing broad-edged nibs for handwriting, calligraphy and posters.

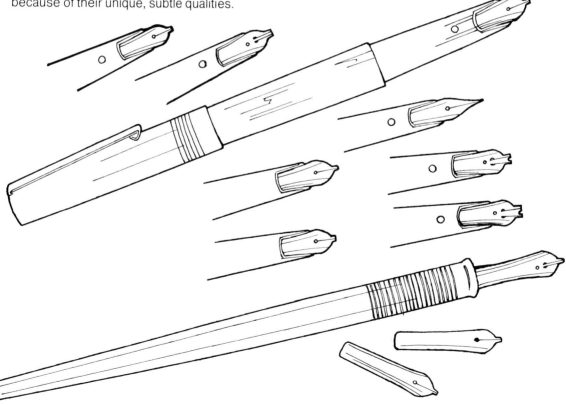

Inks

Fountain pens work on the "controlled-leak" principle. As the nib touches the paper, ink is immediately available for writing. The ink must neither be too thick to clog the delicate feed system nor too thin to flood. Most inks for fountain pens contain solvents to make them free-flowing. You should avoid carbon-based inks and opaque colours which will surely damage your pen.

The colours used by medieval scribes bear little resemblance to fountain pen inks. They were writing with quills and could make their inks as thick and opaque as they liked. By contrast, the colours in fountain pen inks are usually dyes rather than pigments and will sometimes be rather transparent. However, exciting colour schemes can be created with these coloured inks as you will see. Just be careful to select inks which are specially made for your fountain pen, and bear in mind that some inks may fade in direct light.

Paper

To start with you will need paper for practice purposes. Later on you will also need paper for finished work. Unlined layout paper is ideal for practising alphabets and designing roughs. A pad of layout paper is relatively inexpensive and lasts a long time. Most local art shops will also be able to offer you quality machine-made papers for finished work. Choose a smooth, unglazed white or cream paper. As your colour awareness increases you may want to experiment with coloured papers.

When you fill your pen with ink, immerse the nib unit in the ink to cover the nib. While holding the ink converter, push down the plunger to expel the air. As you raise the plunger ink will be drawn into the pen.

You may find keeping an envelope of paper samples a good idea. Only buy one sheet at a time, cut off a small sample piece and note down on it your comments. There is an overwhelming selection of machine-made papers available from specialist paper shops, printers and art shops. By keeping an open mind and experimenting you will soon build up a collection of interesting papers to write on. Handmade papers, parchment and vellum are also used by calligraphers but these are specialist items and very expensive. It is also very difficult to feel relaxed about working on a piece of handmade paper or vellum worth a small fortune!

Making a Good Start

An interesting way of settling down to calligraphy is by creating decorative patterns. If you use shapes from the alphabet you are studying, not only will you reinforce essential pen movements, but the patterns may spark off new ideas for calligraphy designs. A short period of warming up is important, because like piano playing, it helps you to loosen up and relax. Designing patterns can also be quite intriguing.

You will be more comfortable working at a sloping board. Not only does this prevent a distorted view of your work but you will ache less if writing for a long time. Several layers of newsprint covered with cartridge paper on your board improves the writing surface. A guard of paper will protect your work and keep it in place. All your other equipment can be conveniently arranged to one side of the board. If you are right-handed, try to keep your writing paper horizontal as you work. Left-handers may find sloping their paper down to the right more helpful in maintaining the correct pen angle.

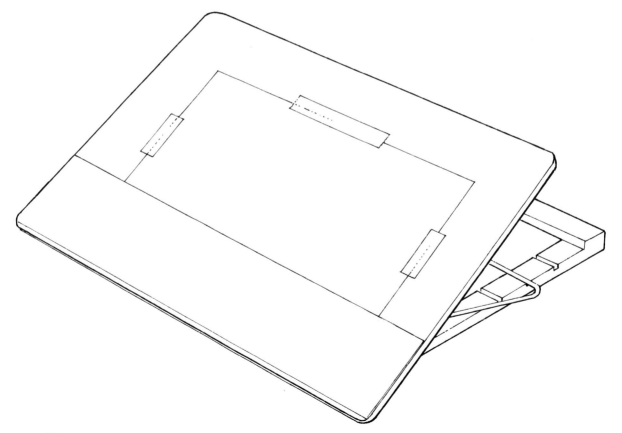

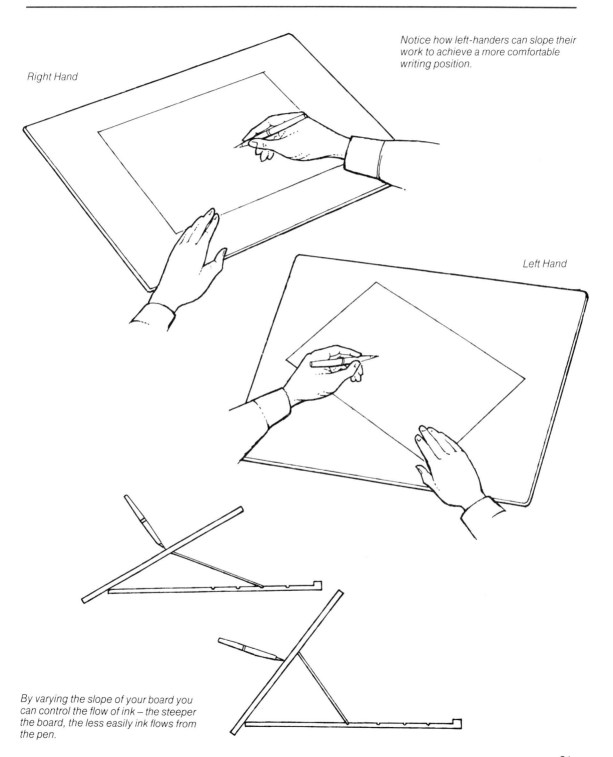

Right Hand

Notice how left-handers can slope their work to achieve a more comfortable writing position.

Left Hand

By varying the slope of your board you can control the flow of ink – the steeper the board, the less easily ink flows from the pen.

Foundational Hand

The Foundational Hand is based on 10th century pen-lettering, notably the Ramsey Psalter which can be seen in the British Library, London. It is a basic script for calligraphers and was developed by Edward Johnston early this century. He used this style for much of his formal penmanship and it is still highly regarded by professional calligraphers today. It makes an excellent alphabet with which to begin and is suited to many applications.

The bold upright appearance and open, circular letter shapes make for easy reading. Our own printing styles were developed in the 15th century from studies of 10th century letters. Notice that each letter shape is built up by following a sequence of movements. The thick and thin strokes are made by holding the pen at an angle to the writing or base line. For this alphabet, the pen angle is 30°, which makes vertical lines heavier than horizontal lines.

Try to maintain the 30° angle as you copy these introductory patterns, which include the most important pen strokes used in constructing this alphabet.

The B4 nib has been used for the decorative patterns and exemplars on this and the following pages. The pen is held at an angle of 30° to the writing line.

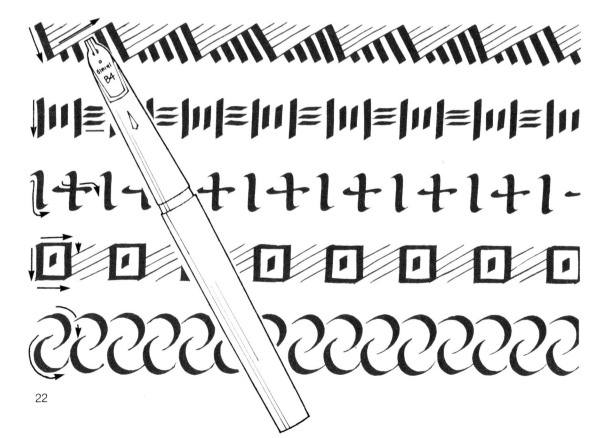

This alphabet of Minuscules and Capitals
makes an excellent starting point. Use a
B4 nib for maximum thick and thin
contrast.

Italic Hand

Another popular alphabet is the Italic style, developed during Renaissance times in Italy. The slight slope to the right and the elliptical appearance of the letter shapes evolved as writing speeds increased. Compared with the Foundational Hand, this style is more elegant and lends itself to flourished strokes, but in forming these flourished letters, be careful not to overdo the twisting lines. An appearance of strangled wrought ironwork is not desirable!

If you intend studying the Italic alphabet you will find the following introductory patterns useful. The horizontal and vertical lines should be equal in thickness. This is achieved by holding the pen at an angle of 45°, halfway between the base line and the perpendicular.

Notice that the horizontal and vertical lines in these patterns are equal in width because the pen is held at an angle of 45° to the writing line.

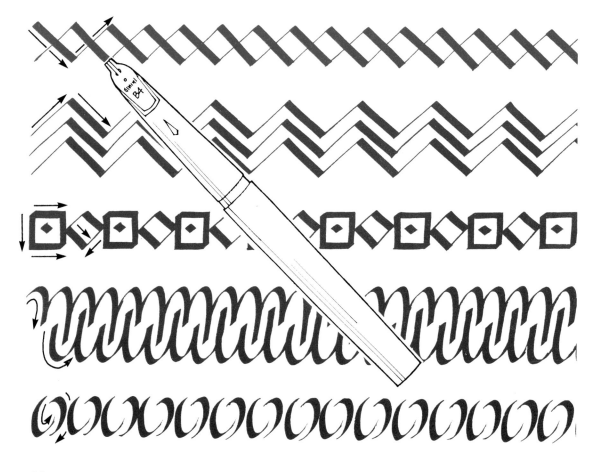

*The alphabet of Italic Capitals and
Minuscules is based on an elliptical 'O'.
All letters slope slightly to the right.*

5 nib widths

abcdefghijklm

nopqrstuvwxyz

ABCDEFGHIJKL

MNOPQRSTUVW

XYZ

FLOURISHED CAPITALS

ABCDEFGHIJKLM

NOPQRSTUVWXYZ

Uncial Hand

These modernised letter shapes owe their origins to bold rounded capitals written between the 5th and 8th centuries. Although most of Europe at this time was under attack from successive waves of warring tribes from Central Asia, small isolated communities of Christian monks continued to work and study in remote parts of Ireland and Northern England.

Two magnificent books have survived from these uncertain times – the Lindisfarne Gospels and the Irish Book of Kells. Both were written by dedicated monks, incredibly knowledgeable about pigments, inks and vellum manufacture. If you can visit the British Library in London you will be able to see the Lindisfarne Gospels for yourself. The Book of Kells is displayed in Trinity College, Dublin. The colours of both books will amaze you. We continue to associate this script with places peopled by Celts and the style is still popular today in Scotland, Ireland and Wales.

By holding the pen square to the writing line you will create very broad vertical lines and very fine horizontal lines. The following patterns help you establish bold letter shapes which are a feature of this alphabet. If you are right-handed, remember to keep your elbow tucked in as you write.

These patterns are made with the pen held square to the writing line, giving broad lines down and fine lines across.

Many calligraphers enjoy this broad upright style. Keep the letters circular and open.

4 nib widths

Gothic Hand

Many people associate the Gothic style of writing with anything "Olde English." It certainly is an old style, having developed in the 12th century and lasted right through medieval times until the 15th century. The style evolved in response to a growing need for economy as the demand for hand-written books increased.

You can see how compressed and narrow the letters are, giving a dense effect of "Black Letters" across the page. Scribes were able to pack far more words to each line and in consequence used less vellum. To relieve these heavy, black letters late-medieval artists designed fine filigree borders, highly coloured and gilded, and often including historiated capitals.

Today, this style is still selected occasionally for house signs, invitations and greetings cards, even though it is not the most legible of scripts. We see so little gothic lettering in print nowadays that you should be cautious when you choose to write this alphabet. Most people find the letters difficult to read so avoid using it for posters or for menus in a dimly-lit restaurant!

The following patterns have been designed to prepare you for the gothic alphabet and feature compressed vertical lines. They will provide useful experience in writing this rigid, angular script. Try to keep your pen at an angle of 40° to the writing line as you work.

Keep your pen between 30° and 40° for these patterns which stress the linear quality of this alphabet.

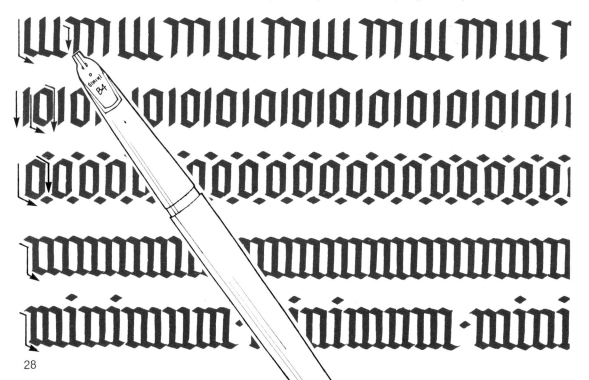

These closely-packed words and lines of lettering give the effect of weaving to this style, hence the name – Textura, to weave.

ditum renocares in cruce in
tem pallus finsti miserere
quesumus animabus on

4 nib widths

a b c d e f g h i j k l m

n o p q r s t u v w x y z

A B C D E F G H I

J K L M N O P Q R

S T U V W X Y Z

Old Manuscripts

Sooner or later I hope you will have the opportunity to visit a museum or library and see original manuscripts for yourself. The more you develop your own calligraphic skills, the more you will appreciate the talents and expertise of medieval scribes, whose work can be a continuing source of inspiration.

In the early stages of your studies, you will probably give manuscripts just a cursory glance, taking in the general appearance of the pages and quickly noting the pen-lettering, coloured capitals and decorative borders. But as your quest for greater knowledge increases, you may find as I do that analysing just one page takes a great deal of time. It is a strange experience looking as closely at a page as the scribe would have done when writing, noticing every mark, every flourish, every line – sometimes even mistakes!

Ruben. frmeon. leui. luda. is sachar. zabulon
et beniamin dan etnepthalim gad etaser
Erant igitur omnefanimaeeorum quaeegrer
faefuntdefemoreiacob feptuaginta quinque
Jofeph autem. inaegrptoerat Quomortuo et
uniuerfif fratrib: eiuf omniq: cognationetua
filu ifrl creuerunt. et quafigerminantefmulti
plicati funt acroboratinimif impleuer terra

tioqi famulatu. tibi feruitutis officia
deferamus : hoc prefertim in tempore
quo religiofarum mentium habitū
ultra parietum oqnatum delegifti.
templum iftud in quo feōq tuoq.

These two pieces of work show studies of original manuscripts. The first is from a page in the Carolingian Grandval Bible, written originally in the 9th century. The second study is from a page in the Metz Pontifical, written in the 14th century and now in the Fitzwilliam Museum, Cambridge.

However, you may not be able to visit museums very often, so studying facsimiles of old manuscripts is another important way of gaining greater colour awareness and an appreciation of calligraphy techniques. Your attempts to copy lettering styles will lead to a better understanding of how the script was constructed and written. Eventually as your expertise increases you will be able to make adaptations to suit your own purposes.

Of course, all this analysis takes time and requires a degree of perseverance, but if you are to progress and gain a greater appreciation of our lettering heritage, studying old manuscripts is very important. It will certainly help to strengthen your judgement, taste and sense of style.

This piece of Italic writing is based on a page from a copy book by the great Italian writing master, Ludovico degli Arrighi. This style, the Chancery Cursive, was very popular in the 16th century and remains so today.

Seguita lo eßempio delle'lre'che pono
ligarfi con tutte'le fue feguenti.in tal mo
do (ioe'

aa ab ac ad ae' af ag ah ai ak al am

an ao ap aq ar as af at au ax ay az

IL medesmo farai con d i k l m n u

Le ligature' poi de' c f s f t formo

le' infra =

scritte'

ct,fa ff fi fm fn fo fr fu fy.

st sf

ff ff ß ft,ta te' ti tm tn to tr tt

COLOUR
SCHEMES

As your ideas about colour develop and your pen skills increase, you will want to begin using colour more effectively in your calligraphy. The following pages display a number of colour projects, which have been included to stimulate your "eye for colour".

The first four projects give detailed, practical instructions, so that anyone, however new to calligraphy, can achieve successful results right from the start. Everyone eventually works out his or her own method of working, so be ready to make changes as you progress. The importance of these initial schemes is to encourage you to begin creating real "Things".

Edward Johnston, who did so much at the beginning of this century to revive interest in calligraphic skills, was emphatic about making "Things". Practicing is vital, of course, but you learn so much in working through a project, however small. You will see imperfections but the finished article will be its own reward.

In addition, as you try out new designs you may like to build up a Colour Scrapbook. This could be a note book or folder filled with scraps of coloured paper, fabrics, magazine cuttings and postcards, ideally with accompanying notes. Include anything which catches your eye. As a source of inspiration this book could prove invaluable in the future, when you branch out and try colour schemes of your own!

A page from my Calligraphy Scrapbook featuring "horizontal line" ideas.

Bookmarks

A successful way to begin using your knowledge of colour
calligraphy is by designing bookmarks. These make personal
inexpensive gifts, and straight away you can combine decorative
patterns with calligraphy to create unique presentations. The
possibilities are endless as the illustrations show.

1. Begin with layout paper and rule out a series of
   rectangles, bookmark size. Check your favourite
   books for suitable lengths.

2. By marking tram-lines down the centre of each rectangle
   you can try out a series of patterns.

3. These can now be copied out carefully onto stiff card
   taking care to rule up with feint lines.

4. By using contrasting background colours with your
   coloured inks, you can create exciting visual effects.

5. To personalise bookmarks, first write a list of names on
   layout paper in the alphabet of your choice. These can
   then be copied onto pre-ruled stiff card and decorative
   patterns added at either end.

6. To make more ambitious designs try including ribbon,
   either as a tassle or threaded through the card.
   Shadow nibs, available from Osmiroid, give an
   interesting twin-line effect and make yet another
   variation for your patterns and calligraphy.

7. If you use even broader nibs, a bookmark can be
   turned into a large nameplate for your door or desk.

Christopher

Thomas

Alexandra

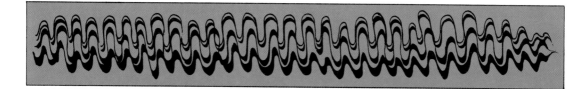

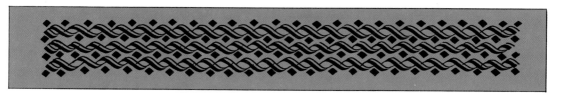

These bookmarks show how the background paper colours can influence the appearance of the patterns and lettering, even to the point where the calligraphy disappears!

Imogen ✦ Imogen

Jessica *from Hebrew meaning 'God beholds.'*

Let your bookcases and your shelves be your gardens & your pleasure grounds. Pluck the fruit that grows therein, gather the roses, the spices & the myrrh.

Harry ✦ Harry

Imogen *may be from the Greek meaning 'beloved child'*

This selection of bookmarks shows how from a very simple beginning you can go on to develop more ambitious designs.

39

Greetings Cards

Everyone enjoys receiving mail, so your next project might be a series of greetings cards to surprise your friends. Keep your designs simple as you start. They will look very effective and you can personalise each one with initials or monograms on the envelopes. The illustrations include designs with decorative patterns, not just in the centre of the card, but making use of the borders. All these ideas help to reinforce pen control and gradually build up your confidence.

1. On layout paper, begin by ruling up a number of rectangles to represent the front of each greetings card. Check that the measurements will allow your cards to fit in their envelopes.

2. Rule tram-lines vertically or horizontally and work out a series of all-over designs, perhaps in two contrasting colours.

3. Diagonal patterns are another possibility and you could include a few words of calligraphy – *HAPPY BIRTHDAY, THANK YOU, BEST WISHES.*

4. If calligraphy is the main feature on your card, any pattern will then play a supporting role. You could try a border pattern but the corners will need special consideration. In order to focus attention on the calligraphy, make sure the pattern colour is toned down.

5. Every element of your card should be carefully considered. The message inside, the choice of coloured inks and card colour, together with the cover design, should all combine to make a pleasing presentation.

6. Now you can transfer all this information to your quality card. This may be difficult to fold, so score the *OUTSIDE* carefully with a craft knife. This gives a professional result and prevents ugly creasing.

7. Your choice of card colour will depend on the recipient – bright primary colours to interest children, zany schemes for teenage friends, subtle colours with colour-related inks to appeal to adults.

8. No two cards need ever be the same and you can be sure that every card will be very well received.

Design idea taken from a Japanese kimono.

Twisted rope pattern.

Log-cabin patchwork design.

Design idea from a Persian manuscript.

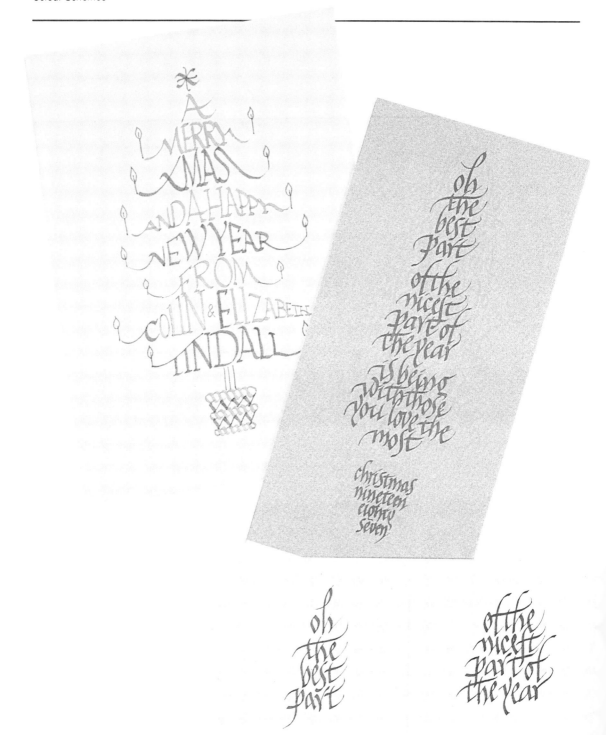

Merry Christmas * Happy New Year

Thank-you

Tiny baby, child divine,
shares his love at Christmastime
from the stable at Bethlehem
across the nations to all men
comes the message that will not cease
all joy be yours, and love and peace.

is being
with those
you love the
most

noel
nineteen
eighty
seven

These greetings cards are from friends interested in calligraphy, who feel as I do, that making cards is a pleasurable and rewarding activity.

43

Invitations

If you are new to calligraphy and have been working through this book, you may now feel ready to tackle a short text. The following ideas for invitations involve a small amount of writing, which could be lettered in either the Foundational or Italic Hand. The lines of lettering are short phrases presented against a decorative left-hand border. One advantage of this type of layout, ranged left, is that you do not need to worry about uneven lengths of lines. As well as having text plus border to consider, you might also be prepared to include larger lettering for the most important line. This will stand out and provide a focal point.

1. Rule up layout paper to your invitation card size, folded either to give a vertical or horizontal design. Adjust measurements to fit the matching envelope.

2. In pencil, sketch out information as short phrases against a vertical line on the left, leaving space for your border pattern.

3. On a separate sheet of layout paper, write out the invitation carefully on continuous lines. Remember to use a broader nib for any large lettering.

4. Now cut up these lines of text with scissors into the short phrases previously selected and arrange these to fit like pieces of a jigsaw.

5. If the short phrases will not fit across the page you may need to use a narrower nib. To help with later designs, keep a note of the nibs you use for each project. This will save you time in the future.

6. Glue these paper strips onto your ruled-up layout paper and complete the decorative border.

7. Now you can sort out your colour scheme. Try and link colours to the occasion for your invitation. Here are some ideas: A multicoloured scheme to suit a firework party; shades of deep red with cream to contrast for a ruby wedding dinner; and how about blue lettering on yellow card for a beach picnic?

8. At last, you are ready to transfer your pen-lettering to the invitation card.

9. Then work on your pattern. Make it a rule always to write first and decorate afterwards, because mistakes to the text can be more difficult to alter.

Decorative Border

You are invited to
the Christening of
Caroline Joanna
at Tusbury Parish Church
on Sunday 4 May at 3pm

RSVP Clare and John Fry
Appleton Lodge, Tusbury

You are invited to
the Christening of
Caroline Joanna
at Tusbury Parish Church
on Sunday 4 May at 3pm

R·S·V·P Clare & John Fry·
Appleton Lodge ·Tusbury·

You are invited to
the Christening of
Caroline Joanna
at Tusbury Parish Church
on Sunday 4 May at 3pm

R·S·V·P Clare & John Fry·
Appleton Lodge ·Tusbury·

Designing monograms is a fascinating exercise. Keep life simple by selecting only two initials. Three or more becomes very complicated!

6-9 · Friday 2 June

Come for Drinks

RSVP ·
Eleanor Shaw
17 Eastways
STEVENTON

~~~~~~~~~~~~~~~~~~~~~~~~~~~~~~~

Your Invitation to the

PENZANCE W·I·

Anniversary Luncheon

~~~~~~~~~~~~~~~~~~~~~~~~~~~~~~~

DISCO

and Supper Party
to celebrate Richard's
Eighteenth Birthday

6-9 · Friday 2 June

Come for Drinks

RSVP ·
Eleanor Shaw
17 Eastways
STEVENTON

Come to a Beach Party

By trying the same colour ink on different coloured backgrounds or different coloured inks on the same background colour, you can create endless colour schemes for your invitations.

Favourite Quotations

You may now feel ready to tackle a more complex presentation, especially if you have worked through the previous ideas. A centred arrangement is a very satisfactory design but needs careful planning and patience. I suggest that you choose a short piece of prose, no more than twenty words or so. Select a nib you feel happy writing with and choose the lettering style which you have practised the most.

You will now need to rule up a series of lines depending on the size of your nib. Ruling lines is a necessary part of calligraphy. The measuring and ruling does take time, but if you regard the activity as part of the "tuning-up" process, you will be altogether better prepared. I find a technical pencil helps to keep all the lines very fine.

1. On layout paper rule lines the body-height of your chosen alphabet, allowing double space between for ascenders and descenders.

2. Carefully write out the quotation, paying particular attention to letter shapes, spacing between letters and spacing between words.

3. Now with a pencil divide up the text into suitable phrases. You could take a number of photocopies at this stage before cutting up the text.

4. On a clean sheet of paper, mark a vertical central line. Cut up the text into the strips of appropriate phrases. Fold each strip in half and lay over the centre line.

5. Once you have achieved a satisfactory presentation, paste these pieces in place.

6. One phrase may be more important and so you could rewrite this in a broader nib to provide a focal point.

7. Look at the overall symmetrical shape of your text. Does it look satisfactory and comfortable on the page? Have you allowed generous margins around the text?

8. Finally plan your colour scheme, choosing inks and paper sympathetic to your quotation.

9. Now you can write out the text onto the good paper but do not be dismayed if you are not entirely satisfied with your first effort. You may need to make further adjustments and copy the piece again. Getting it right first time is rare!

I hear and I forget.
I see and I remember.
I do and I understand.

CHINESE PROVERB

I hear and I forget.
I see and I remember.
I do and I understand.

CHINESE PROVERB

I hear and I forget.
I see and I remember.
I do and I understand.

CHINESE PROVERB

I hear and I forget.
I see and I remember.
I do and I understand.

CHINESE PROVERB

See how the amount of margin influences the appearance of the text on the page.

By pasting your pen-lettering over a central vertical line, you will achieve a symmetrical presentation.

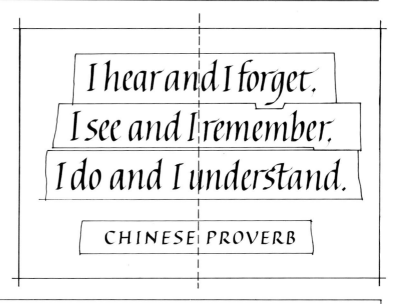

I hear and I forget,
I see and I remember,
I do and I understand.

CHINESE PROVERB

The use of two pieces of mounting board, cut at a right angle, helps in deciding how much margin to leave when the finished work is framed.

More Advanced Projects

The following selection of calligraphy shows you more detailed presentations, which all require considerable planning. However, the method of working is just the same as described in the previous pages. Initial roughs are worked out in pencil on layout paper, sketching in any illustration or decoration needed. Preliminary drafts are made in pen to sort out design problems. It is important at this stage to experiment with changes of letter height and weight. Every stage in the development of a piece of work is crucial, allowing you time to evaluate your intentions. This refining process may result in many trials, before you start on the final piece.

I have included in this selection pieces of work which exhibit traditional features associated with calligraphy. Scrolls, loyal addresses, testimonials and family trees are all projects which can include heraldic art and gilding. These are areas of advanced study, but they greatly increase the potential for creating exciting colour schemes. Even today two or three specialists sometimes combine on a major piece of work, just as scribes did in medieval times. One will write the text, another will do all the gilding and a third will paint all the illustrations or heraldry.

The other pieces of calligraphy in this selection show how the texts can be interpreted more freely. Why not experiment, as I have done, with inks and paints to produce your own exciting background papers? These can be marbled, or by wetting the paper first, can exhibit blurred and cloudy effects. You can also try diluting your inks to make subtle gradations of colour within the lettering.

I hope you will visit calligraphy exhibitions and see for yourself just how exciting interpretive calligraphy can be. However, like other crafts you can only achieve spontaneity and freedom in your work once you have acquired expertise in penmanship.

The Duke Family Tree is a major project, requiring many hours of planning. 100cm × 90cm Gouache and stick ink on vellum.

PEDIGREE OF DUKE

BLAZON

ARMS · Tierce in pairle sable gules
and azure three chaplets of roses or.
+ + + + + + + + + +
CREST · On a wreath sable and or
issuant from the battlements of a
tower azure a demi griffin or beak-
ed and membered gules holding a
+ chaplet of roses also azure +

DESCRIPTION

ARMS · The field is partitioned into three, black, red and blue, each +
with a wreath of gold roses. + + +
CREST · On a black & gold wreath +
rising from the battlements of a blue
tower, a gold half griffin (half lion
half eagle) with a red beak and red
legs holding a wreath of blue roses. +

GRADATIM · VINCIMUS

John Duke ÷ Olive Cradle
of Tottington in the parish of Lyminster, co· Sussex, 1640/1. Buried there 29 March 1645. | Married 6 May 1606 at Lyminster afsd. Buried there 11 November 1637.

Thomas Duke ÷ Elizabeth Cobden | **Jone** | **Ellen** | **Alice**
of Warningcamp in the parish of Lyminster aforesaid. Baptised 25 December 1608. | Married 20 April 1630 at Lyminster afsd. Buried there 12 April 1651. | Baptised 22 March 1606/7 at Lyminster aforesaid. | Baptised 26 July 1612. | Baptised 23 April 1615.

Mary ÷ **John Duke** ÷ **Sarah**
daughter of . . . Leggatt, widow of Richard Oliver of Tottington afsd. Married 11 July 1674 at Yapton, co· Sussex. Buried 21 June 1679 at Lyminster afsd. | of Lyminster aforesaid. Buried there 20 March 1692. | dau' of Thomas Upperton, of Tottington afsd. and widow of Thomas Gardiner of Burpham, co. Sussex. Married December or January 1679/80. Buried 25 January 1721 at Lyminster, aged 72.

Thomas Duke ÷ Ann Bridger
of Littlehampton, co· Sussex. Baptised 16 November 1680 at Lyminster afsd. Buried 11 January 1732/3 at Littlehampton. Admon 14 July 1733 to his widow, Chichester. | of Tillington, co. Sussex. Marriage Licence at Chichester dated 1 May 1703, married same month at Lugarshall, co· Sussex. Admix of her husband 1733. Buried 4 December 1748 at Littlehampton.

James Duke ÷ Elizabeth | **Thomas Duke ÷ Ann Francis** | **Henry Duke** | **Other Issue**
of Week in Lyminster afsd. Baptised 2 March 1705/4 at Littlehampton. Buried there 27 January 1751/2. Will dated 20 Jan. 1751/2 Proved at Chichester. | sister of Henry Postlewaite, ment'd 1751/2. Buried 4 Sept. 1750 at Littlehampton afsd. Will dated 16 April 1748, proved 22 Sept. 1750 at Chichester. | of Week in Lyminster afsd. Yeoman. Baptised 16 January 1707/8 at Littlehampton. Will dated 5 Feb. 1761, proved 6 Jan. 1762 at Chichester. | of Littlehampton afsd. Marriage Licence at Chichester 1 February 1734/5. Ment'd in her husband's will 1761. | of Littlehampton afsd. Yeoman. Baptised there 9 Oct. 1720. Buried there 1 February 1747/8. Will dated 7 Dec. 1746 proved at Chichester.

John Duke | **James Duke ÷ Jane Blake** | **Richard Thomas George Henry Isaac** | **Ann** | **Elizabeth**
Eldest son. Mentioned in the wills of his grandmother, Ann, 1747 and father, 1761. | of Littlehampton afsd. Yeoman, ment'd in the wills of his grandmother 1747 and father, 1761. Will dated 17 Feb. 1808, proved 5 October 1808 at Chichester. | of Littlehampton afsd. Marriage Licence 11 Nov. 1785 at Chichester afsd. Ment'd in her husband's will 1808. | **Duke Duke Duke Duke Duke** All mentioned 1761. | Mentioned in her grandmother's | Mentioned in the wills of her aunt

James Duke Richard Duke Thomas Duke | **William Duke ÷ Anne or Ann**
All mentioned in their fathers will 1808. | of Steyning, co. Sussex. Mentioned in his fathers will 1808. Buried 27 November 1859 aged 46 at Lyminster afsd. Will dated 28 February 1854, proved 24 January 1840 at Chichester. | dau' of Robert Aysh... Sussex. Baptised ther... married by licence ... February 1867 at L...

Ayshford Duke | **Thomas Duke ÷ Harriet**
Mentioned in his fathers will 1854. | of Steyning afsd. Baptised there 12 June 1832. Died there 10 June 1916. | dau' of Thomas Trusler. Marr... February 1862 at St. Nicholas, B... aged 28. Died 3 August 1911. B... Steyning aforesaid.

James Duke ÷ Mary Mildred
of Worthing, co· Sussex. Born 19 May 1875 at Steyning afsd. Died at Worthing 4 October 1958. | dau' of William Powell Breach of Newnham, St... afsd. Born 17 April 1880 at Steyning. Married ther... October 1903. Died 3 January 1951. Buried at Bisho... Waltham, co. Southampton.

Thomas James Duke ÷ Eileen Winifred
of Curdridge Croft, Curdridge, co· Southampton. In the Commission of the Peace for co · Southampton. Born 12 November 1907 at Bishops Waltham aforesaid. | commonly known as Anne, dau' of Walter Frank... Daley of Etheldon Read, Shepherd's Bush, co· Londo... Married at Christchurch, Lancaster Gate, co· Lon... 10 June 1937.

Thomas James ÷ Sarah Jane Nicholas Duke | **Alan Hugh Keep ÷ Jennifer Edwards** | **Julian Huber... Harvey**
of Scdham House, Droxford, co· Hampshire. Born 26 June 1945 at Fishers Pond, Eastleigh, co. Southampton. | dau' of Commander D.L. Syms of Wickham, co· Hants. Born 25 October 1955 at Fareham, co· Southampton. Married 7 June 1975 at St Nicholas Church, Wickham. | of Homestead Farm, Galley Hill, Selborn, near Alton, co· Hants. Born 16 September 1956 at Banstead, co Surrey. | Born 13 June 1959 at Bishops Waltham afsd. Married 23 April 1960 at St. Peter's Church, Bishops Waltham afsd. | of Yew Tree Cottage, Th... Godalming, Surrey. Bor... June 1958 at Dorchest... Dorset.

Cordelia Mary | Felicity Clare | Iona Harriet | **Paul Anthony Robert James Karen Elizabeth Keep Edwards Keep Edwards Keep** | **Camilla Lucy Keep**
Born 29 September 1976. Born 8 May 1978. Born 11 February 1982. All born at Royal County Hospital, Winchester, co· Hants. | Born 10 August 1961. Born 14 August 1965. Born 2 October 1962. All born at Royal County Hospital, Winchester, co. Hants. | Born 6 September 196... at Aldershot General Hospital, co. Hants.

GRADATIM · VINCIMUS

Churches often have subdued lighting, making legibility an important factor. I selected black lettering on off-white vellum for maximum contrast, a Foundational Hand style for easy reading, and picked out keywords in red to provide variety.
50cm × 70cm Gouache and stick ink on vellum.

Bugo Mauduyt
de Knoville
Richard de Alresford
Robert Hyblethwatt
John atte Brigge

✝1253 ⋎ John de Horsia   ⚜ ⋎ 1495 ⋎
✝1290 ⋊ ◊ Bogo de Cnovile   ⚜ ✝ 1495 ⋊ ⟍
✝1305 ⋊ ✝ Richard de Alresford ⚜ ⋎ 1495 ⋊ ⌄
✝1315 ✝ ⋎ Bugo Mauduyt   ⚜ ⋎ 1495 ⋊ ⌄
✝
✝   ❘

by 1253   John de Horsia   ⋊ 1556   John Jacklyn
✤ 1290   Bogo de Cnovile   by 1562   William Ricard
✤ 1305   Richard de Alresford   ⋊ 1599   John Pildrym
✤ 1315   Bugo Mauduyt de e e e ⋊ 1599   John Prowse · minister
✤   de Knoville   ⋊ 1253   ∴∴
✤ 1305   1963   ⋊ 1253
∴ 1234   1253   ⋊ 1253
∴ 1234   1290   ⋊ 1305
∴ 1963   1305   ⋊ 1562
✤   1315   ⋊ 1978

RECTORS · OF · GRATELEY · WITH · QUARLEY
RECTORS · OF · CRATELEY · WITH · QUARLEY
AND ·

Remember · them · who · have · spoken · unto · you · the · words · of · eternal · Life.

⌒ Remember them who have spoken unto you the words of eternal life

RECTORS · OF · ST · LEONARD'S

AMPORT; GRATELEY; MONXTON · AND · QUARLEY

RECTORS · OF · GRATELEY · WITH · QUARLEY

INCUMBENTS · OF · BENEFICE · OF · AMPORT; GRATELEY · & QUARLEY

Remember them who have spoken unto you words of the eternal life.

·RECTORS·OF·ST·LEONARD'S· ·GRATELEY·

by1253	John de Horsia	✢1554	Robert Hyblethwatt
✢1290	Bogo de Cnovile	✢1556	John Jacklyn
✢1305	Richard de Alresford	by1562	William Ricard
✢1315	Bugo Mauduyt de	✢1599	John Pildrym
✢ ✢ ✢	Knoville	✢1604	James Samborn
✢1318	Bugo Mauduyt	✢1613	Thomas South
✢1330	William de Chece	✢1625	John Langley
✢1332	John de Bury	✢1641	Richard South
✢1333	Thomas Geraud	in 1654	John Prowse · minister
✢1333	William Burel	in 1659	Robert Long · minister
✢1339	John atte Brigge	✢1660	Philip Baker
✢1340	William Rydel	✢1691	Thomas Derby
✢1361	William Payn	✢1699	Richard Jenks
✢1363	John Bradeford	✢1731	James Smith
✢1368	Hugh Wryghte	✢1737	George Strother
✢1400	William Gyles	✢1764	Henry Courthope
✢1401	John Clere	✢1773	George Woodward
✢1402	Richard Puendre	✢1787	Richard Turner
✢1413	Robert Guerad	✢1819	Christopher Dodson
✢ ✢ ✢	(missing register)	✢1876	William Stone
by1490	John Waterend	✢1879	Thomas John Whitworth
✢1490	John Cooke	✢1884	Frederick de Paravicini
by1533	William Perkyns	✢1904	Frederick James Fuller
✢1533	Edmund Mordaunt	✢1920	Daniel Henry Moore
✢1539	Thomas Ponnell	✢1925	Reginald H·A·Currey

RECTORS·OF·GRATELEY·WITH·QUARLEY

✢1931	Reginald H·A·Currey	✢1959	Cyril Brundritt
✢1946	Adam Lawton		

INCUMBENTS·OF·BENEFICE·OF·AMPORT·GRATELEY·AND·QUARLEY

✢1969	George S·G·Stokes	✢1975	Christopher Tayler

INCUMBENTS·OF·AMPORT·GRATELEY·MONXTON·AND·QUARLEY

✢1978	Michael John Grylls

✢ ✢ Remember them who have spoken unto you the words of eternal life. ✢ ✢

Barbara Bundy · 1985·

Studies of manuscripts provide inspiring sources for design ideas. This illustration was taken from a 12th century manuscript and shows St. Luke the Evangelist, seated on a bull, which is his symbol.

Know all men by these Presents that We the Council of the
CITY OF WINCHESTER
in consideration of the eminent services rendered by her
to the City and to the Council have granted and by these
Presents do grant and confirm unto

BARBARA DOROTHY MARY
CARPENTER TURNER
B.A., F.R.Hist.S., J.P.

the Honorary Freedom of the City of Winchester.

In Witness whereof we have caused our Common Seal to be hereunto
affixed this first day of August one thousand nine hundred and
eighty seven in the presence of

MAYOR   CHIEF EXECUTIVE

*A scroll made of vellum is traditionally used
for Loyal Addresses and Testimonials,
usually protected by a scroll case. The
design often involves a heraldic device
with the text, and space underneath for a
seal and signatures.*

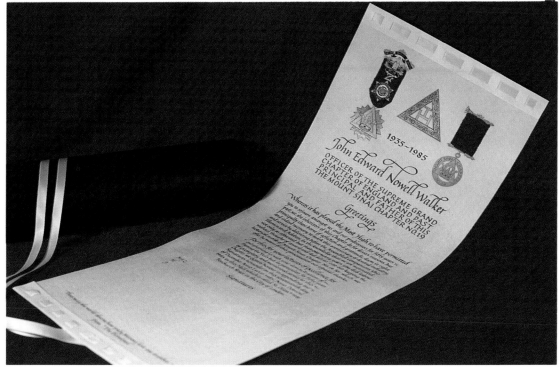

When you are old and grey and full of sleep,
And nodding by the fire, take down this book,
And slowly read, and dream of the soft look
Your eyes had once, and of their shadows deep;

How many loved your moments of glad grace,
And loved your beauty with love false and true,
But one man loved the pilgrim soul in you,
And loved the sorrows of your changing face;

And bending down beside the glowing bars,
Murmur, a little sadly, how Love fled
And paced upon the mountain overhead
And hid his face amid a crowd of stars.

· W H E N   Y O U   A R E   O L D ·   W · B · Y E A T E S ·

The fluid, undulating lines were chosen for this piece to convey the dreamy mood of the poem. There are no defined borders because drowsiness is a half-sleep, half-waking condition. The grey lettering provides a softer appearance to the lines, contributing to the dream-like atmosphere.

*This is also a very quiet piece – calm
morning – and I decided to allow the
words to speak for themselves, again in
shades of grey for quietness.*

Calm is the morn without a sound.
  Calm as to suit a calmer grief.
  And only thro' the faded leaf
The chesnut pattering to the ground:

Calm and deep peace on this high wold,
  And on these dews that drench the furze,
  And all the silvery gossamers
That twinkle into green and gold:

from IN MEMORIAM · TENNYSON

Try using ink and water colour washes for experimental backgrounds. Damp the paper first for explosive effects. Dip a sponge in diluted ink for interesting textures. These papers can then be used for any of the introductory projects.

An interpretative experiment where four lines of lettering are colour-graded to achieve a more interesting effect.

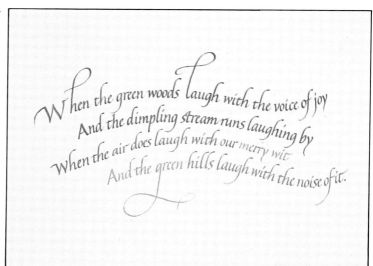

When the green woods laugh with the voice of joy
And the dimpling stream runs laughing by
When the air does laugh with our merry wit
And the green hills laugh with the noise of it.

Hand-marbled paper provided the inspiration for this piece of calligraphy – the lettering follows the lines of marbling and the undulations suggest the movement of the sea.

I must go down to the sea again
to the lonely sea and the sky,
And all I ask is a tall ship
and a star to steer her by.

Designing for Colour Calligraphy

Once you have tried some of the projects in this book, you will want to develop your own calligraphy ideas. How do you set about this?

First you must consider carefully the piece of prose or poetry you intend to write out, reading through the text several times. To avoid muddled thinking, be quite clear about your intentions. Do you want to let the words speak for themselves, or do you intend to create a more personal interpretation? Have you considered where the piece of work will be viewed? Are there any circumstances which may affect the size of lettering and legibility?

The ideas that come to mind can be quickly jotted down. You may find, as I do, that some time is needed to plan your design, sketching out initial roughs in pencil. Then the arrangement of the text can be worked out using an appropriate script, also experimenting with different sizes of pen-lettering.

If the information is lengthy, the design may need to be divided up into a number of different elements. You must decide how much importance to give each one. You may have a main text area, smaller areas of information, a large initial capital perhaps, or a bold heading in capitals. All these elements must be carefully arranged to arrive at a pleasing unity. You will find it easier to work on each section at a time and paste them together afterwards.

Finally, you must decide on a colour scheme, which may include the frame, mounting card, background paper and coloured inks. Sometimes it is easier to choose a suitable moulding first, so that you can link all your coloured inks and paper to the frame. Your colour scrapbook will also be a useful source of inspiration, particularly if you have a number of colour schemes in mind.

Having worked through all these stages, only now will you be ready to write out the final piece. In all your calligraphic designing, I hope you will be helped by asking yourself the following questions:

1. Have you done justice to the text?
2. Have you interpreted the author's intentions?
3. Does the selected script complement the text?
4. Have you remembered that the simpler the design the more likely it is to be successful?

CONCLUSION

As time goes by, you may want to join a local calligraphy class and share your ideas with others. You will be able to sort out any problems, contribute to group discussions and watch demonstrations by the tutor. Classes at local Adult Education Institutes are often held weekly. Residential education centres also offer weekend and week courses, where you can study aspects of calligraphy in depth.

You may also like to join a calligraphy society. Your region may have a group of calligraphers who meet monthly, inviting guest speakers and arranging museum visits. These societies help you keep in touch with ideas, exhibitions, articles of interest and details about equipment. There is nothing worse than working in isolation, so even if there are no local classes, society newsletters can help spur you on. Further information about calligraphy societies in this country and abroad is listed on page 64.

I hope you will find the ideas in this book useful and I wish you every success in your calligraphy studies. Remember, no practice is ever a waste of time, but too much practice is not a good thing! Why not start a small piece of colour calligraphy you aim to finish today – a card to a relative, a favourite verse to give to your friend or perhaps a bookmark for yourself? You will be rewarded with a real sense of satisfaction and achievement.

Osmiroid Creative Leisure Series

Each title in the Osmiroid Creative Leisure series has been written in a lively "to the point" style, with very practical advice to ensure that exciting creative results are quickly achievable.

Chinese Brush Painting includes Chinese Calligraphy and a host of ideas from animal and plant subjects to landscapes.

Pen and Ink Drawing leads the reader through many subjects and styles and includes enough "tricks of the trade" to ensure that everyone can create something.

The Art of Sketching shows the reader how to approach sketching from a very practical viewpoint, covering a wide range of indoor and outdoor subjects.

The Art of Poster Making shows the reader how to create posters using the wide variety of media and ideas.

The Art of Stencilling gives the reader all they need to know to stencil onto walls, fabrics, furniture or paper, with manufactured or home made stencils.

Calligraphy Societies

The Society of Scribes and Illuminators
Honorary Secretary, 54 Boileau Road, London SW13 9BL

The Society for Italic Handwriting
The Secretary, 80 Greenleaf Gardens, Polegate, East Sussex BN26 6PH

Calligraphy North
c/o Brian Walker, 32 Braemar Croft, South Hiendley, Barnsley, Yorks S72 9DB

North East Scribes
c/o Rev R Cooper, The Rectory, Middleton Road, Sadberge, Darlington, Co. Durham D22 1RP

South Bank Scriveners
c/o Tony Curtis, Rose Cottage, 9 Station Road, Great Coates, Grimsby DN37 9NP

North Downs Calligraphers
c/o Patricia Lovett, Hernewood, Gracious Lane, Sevenoaks, Kent TN13 1TJ

Oxford Scribes
c/o David Nicholls, University Museum, Parks Road, Oxford OX1 3PB

West Country Scribes
c/o Malcolm Drake, 29 Oak Grove, Cheddar, Somerset BS27 3BW

Australian Society of Calligraphers
P.O. Box 184, West Ryde 2114, AUSTRALIA

Bow Valley Calligraphers
P.O. Box 1647, Station M, Calgary, Alberta T2P 2L7, CANADA

Calligraphy Arts Guild of Toronto
P.O. Box 115, Willowdale Station A, Willowdale, Ontario, M2N 5S7, CANADA

Scriptores
P.O. Box 331, 9100AH, Dokkum, HOLLAND

Norwegian Calligraphy Society
c/o Bas Vlam, Kalligrafisk, Verksted, 3730 Ulefoss, NORWAY

Society for Calligraphy and Italic Handwriting
P.O. Box 34481, Jettestown 2043, SOUTH AFRICA

Friends of Calligraphy
P.O. Box 5194, San Francisco CA94101, U.S.A.

Washington Calligraphers Guild
Box 23818, Washington D.C. 20024, U.S.A.

Society of Scribes
P.O. Box 933, New York City NY10022, U.S.A.

Society for Calligraphy
P.O. Box 64174, Los Angeles CA90064, U.S.A.

Houston Calligraphy Guild
c/o Art League of Houston, 1953, Montrose, Houston, Texas 77006, U.S.A.

Colleagues of Calligraphy
P.O. Box 4024, Saint Paul, Minneapolis 55104, U.S.A.

Western American Branch of the S.I.H.
6800 S.E. 32nd Avenue, Portland, Oregon 97202, U.S.A.

Acknowledgements

Special thanks to Mrs Sybil Bunn, Mrs Barbara Carpenter Turner, Mrs. Chris Haslett, Mr Tom Duke and Mr Viv Williams, who have kindly loaned commissioned pieces for inclusion in this book. Also grateful thanks to my husband Paul for his encouragement and assistance.

Design and artwork by Nigel Long, Winchester